Trying it Gods way

Your life will forever be changed

Natalie Eleanor

ISBN 978-93-5610-646-8
© Natalie Eleanor 2022
Published in India 2022 by Pencil

A brand of

One Point Six Technologies Pvt. Ltd.
123, Building J2, Shram Seva Premises,
Wadala Truck Terminal, Wadala (E)
Mumbai 400037, Maharashtra, INDIA
E connect@thepencilapp.com
W www.thepencilapp.com

CONTENTS

Acknowledgements

First and foremost I would like to thank my Heavanly father for my salvation and for making it possible for me to inspire others who will be reading this book. All the praise and glory belongs to God. Then there's my best friend and partner, Michael. Thank you for your love and support, i love you always. To our children, we love you dearly.

Introduction

Have you ever wondered what would happen if we all lived according to God's word? How would our lives have turned out? (Matthew 4:4) - Jesus answered, "it is written: 'man shall not live on bread alone, but on every word that comes from the mouth of God". It is strange that we live in a world where we do exactly the opposite of what God requires from us.

Some of us know the truth but we still choose to live a life without God. Scripture teaches us to seek first the Kingdom of God and live righteously and He will give us everything we need. (Matthew 6:33)

My past experiences and what God has done in my life, inspired me to write this book, with a lot of guidance from above, my special somebody and a little help from some amazing preachers across the world, watching their sermons, getting a better understanding of the Word. I hope this book will inspire, guide, and encourage everyone to seek God first and to live a life that pleases him. May it help you connect with God on a deeper, spiritual level.

It is only through knowing Him that you can find fulfillment and peace in your relationship with God, yourself, and others.

We live in a world where everything (or most of the things) we do, goes against the will of God for our lives. We do so many things on a daily basis that does not please

God. We do not even realize it. Some of us just choose not to obey. How many times have we not gone into situations without praying about it, where did it lead us? Have you ever wondered why some of the decisions you made did not work out or why it did not last? Was God in that situation? Did you pray about it? Putting God first above anything else is the only way to live a happy, fulfilled, and blessed life.

May this book help you understand what God's plan for your life is.

For I know the plans I have for you, plans to prosper you and not to harm you, plans to give you hope and a future. Jeremiah 29:11

Chapter one

"Knowing who you are"

You can only truly know who you are if you know God.
Knowing who you are means to always be true to yourself,
Standing firm in your beliefs, setting affirmations, and
living by them.
 Many of us are just settlers, meaning we settle for most
things in our lives. We think what we get is what we need
to be content with. That is not living a fulfilled life. We do
not need to lower our standards in order to find someone
to love, we simply must be ourselves. Being true to
yourself means knowing exactly what you want and waiting
for it. It is only in knowing who you are that you can love
yourself and it is only in loving yourself that you can love
others.
 God has made each one of us unique in our way, we all
have a purpose but first we need to love God, love
ourselves and then love others.

Who am I?

(Psalm 139:14) I praise you, for I am fearfully and
wonderfully made.
If translated from Hebrew fearfully means heartfelt-
interest and respect.

That is exactly how God sees us and what He had in mind when He created us.

We are so special in God's eyes, each, and every one of us. Why should we think any less of ourselves and feel the need to settle?

John 3:16 For God so loved the world that He gave His only begotten son.

Heartfelt interest: - He loved us so much, so we ought to love ourselves and others equally.

Respect: - God thought highly of us even before we were formed in the womb,

(Jeremiah 1:15) He created us for a purpose. We ought to respect God, ourselves, and others. We respect God by living according to His word, turning away from anything that does not please Him, putting Him first in everything we do. Obeying His commandments. We respect ourselves by doing good and believing in ourselves. We respect others by showing humility and kindness.

Wonderfully made: - Hebrew translation, unique and set apart. In other words, you were created with great reverence. God set you apart because He has a great purpose for you and only you. No one else can do what God has called you to do.

Your unique identity

1.   Authenticity (being yourself/real) will expose your real allies. Some people are attached to a version of you that is not the real you.

2.   When you are being real it will reveal to you those

who are really for you and assigned to you.

3.   God will not divinely join you with someone who you cannot be yourself with.

4.   Being real increases your anointing.

5.   God's anointing only falls on the real you. He will not anoint who you pretend to be.

What does it mean to have the anointing of God on your life?

To be anointed means to be set apart, empowered, or protected. To be set apart means to keep or save (something) for a particular purpose. That is why you cannot be anyone other than yourself. The word holy in Hebrew is kadash – which also means to be set apart for a specific task. So being anointed means that we are holy. It does not mean that we need to be perfect, it simply means that you are important.

Fear not, for I have redeemed you; I have summoned you by name, you are mine. Isaiah 43:1

Chapter two

"Living a life of prayer"

Praying is our way of talking to God. Why is it so important to talk to God? He is the Author and Finisher of our faith. (Hebrews 12:2) meaning God is in complete control of our lives, He knows the beginning and He knows how it is going to end. By praying, we seek God's presence, we seek guidance and wisdom, because we believe in a power greater than us. Prayer keeps us from living a sinful life by abiding by God's word. The Bible (law).

We are all familiar with the ten commandments, but how many of us actually abide by them? How many of these commandments do we apply to our lives? Because we are all human, we fall short of God's glory. That is why we pray and ask for forgiveness for our sins. No prayer goes unheard, we simply have to trust God's timing. Mark 11:25 and when you stand praying, if you hold anything against anyone, forgive them, so that your Father in heaven may forgive you your sins.

When it comes to choosing a life partner, it is best to pray about it and wait on God. It is so easy to just settle and take what is readily available. You will meet the right person at the right time. Find God and the right person will find you.

How do you find God? It is actually very simple. Pray. Seek Him. John 16:23-24 very truly I tell you, my Father will give you whatever you ask in My name. Until now you have not asked for anything in My name. Ask and you will receive, and your joy will be complete.

God sees and He knows our hearts. He provides us with what we need even before we ask Him. (Matthew 6:8)

But God needs us to seek Him, ask Him, He wants us to reach out to Him, it is up to us to take that step. Revelation 3:26 Behold I stand at the door and knock, if any man hears my voice and open the door. (Take that step, make that choice) I will come into him and will sup with him and He with me.

Prayer changes things. So many times, we try to do things on our own, but for how long does it last? The things that this world has to offer are just temporary but God can give us eternal life.

Doing the right thing is never easy, so is waiting for the right one, but giving up and settling for less, leads to a life of misery and heartache.

But when you pray, you must believe and not doubt at all. Whoever doubts is like a wave in the sea that is driven and blown about by the wind.James 1:6-7

Chapter Three

"Overcome the enemy"

When we devote our lives to Christ, we are often faced with a lot of challenges. The enemy knows there is greatness within us, and he will try everything to distract, derail or discourage us. He will even cause frustration. It is also better known as attacks from the enemy. How do we overcome these attacks? By praying and seeking the presence of God.

Ephesians 6:11 Put on the full Armor of God, so that you will be able to stand firm against the schemes of the devil. What is the full Armor of God? Stand firm with the Belt of Truth around your waist, knowing you are safe and secure with the Breastplate of Righteousness guarding your heart from evil, helping you live a life that honors God. Put on the Gospel Shoes of Faith, so you are protected against Satan's fiery darts of lies, fear and deceit. Place on your head the Helmet of Salvation, keeping your mind focused on God. Grab hold in your hand the Sword of The Spirit, the Word of God, sharp and true.

Corinthians 15:58 Be steadfast, immovable, always abounding in the work of the Lord. We need to be more Christlike. Do what God would do. Because we are human, we need to reach out to a power greater than us. God's word reminds us that we are not alone. Hebrews 13:

5 He will never leave nor forsake us. So, in our times of trials and tribulations, when we are feeling at our lowest, when the enemy tries to convince us that we are weak and helpless, we know that we can call on God in times of trouble and He will sustain us. He is the source of our strength.

The enemy (Satan) is a master manipulator of the mind. His job is to plant seeds of doubt, fear, anxiety in our minds but it is up to us whether we are going to water those seeds and allow them to grow or wither. One of the enemy's tactics is to bring confusion and to cloud our minds. That is why whenever we pray, we ask God to grant us wisdom. Nothing that God sends comes without confirmation.

Our greatest blessing comes from our obedience to God. Knowing God is to do His will, to fully trust Him and commit our lives to Him.

Learn to fight with spiritual weapons. Ephesians 6:12, For our struggle is not against flesh and blood but against the rulers, against the authorities, against the powers of this dark world and against the spiritual forces of evil in the heavenly realms.

How do we go into spiritual warfare?
By praying, calling on the Name of the Lord. Luke 10:19 Behold I have given you authority to tread on serpents and scorpions and over all the power of the enemy and nothing shall in any way hurt you.

We already have this power; God has placed it within us. Sometimes we do not realize how much power we have through Jesus Christ, and we allow the devil to convince us otherwise by telling us we are weak, we will never make it, he reminds us of our past, and this causes us to doubt ourselves and to have a fear of the future. 2 Timothy 1:7 But God has not given us a spirit of fear but of power, and love and of a sound mind. The devil despises marriage and family, he causes destruction, chaos and division. Because of this most of us came from broken homes, foster homes and the absenteeism of one parent in a home. This is why it is so vital to know God and to seek Him daily, and to read His word, this is how we defeat the enemy.

This is why we should always continuously pray for our families. We always hear the phrase, a family that prays together, stays together and there is so much truth in that.

Our lives are made up from a bundle of choices. Whichever direction we choose in life, which is where we end up. We need to make good choices, set standards for ourselves and live by them. Success is the result of our decisions. So is failure.

Choose to live a life that pleases God. Put Him first in everything you do. Choose to wait on God. Isaiah 40:13 says that those who wait upon the Lord shall renew their strength. Draw strength from God, apply His word to your life daily. Matthew 6:33 Seek first the Kingdom of God and live righteously and He will give you everything you need.

Jesus gives us the assurance that He has given us the power to overcome all the power of the enemy, and nothing shall harm us. Luke 10:19

Chapter Four

'Relationship Goals'

What God desires from us, is that we love Him above anything else. It is the most important relationship each and every one of us needs in our lives before we can have any other relationships. The scripture, 'Seek first the Kingdom of God', refers to us putting God first in all we do, that includes, praying about any situation before we attempt to face it. Being available for God first, should be our number one priority. There is a saying that goes: "Worry is in your space, because your priorities are out of place". When God is first in your life, you do not need to worry about anything. God has you covered and even when you are facing difficulties, just know that He is always there. Giving you strength and the necessary wisdom to overcome.

Many of us, in our relationships, at some point, feel lost. That is because we do not seek God's guidance. I speak from experience when I say, I have been down this road. I have tried to do things on my own, and in my own way, a couple of times. Even making some decisions on the impulse. Because I felt the need to fit in and to belong. All I got out of it was a lot of pain, heartbreak and disappointment. I led a life of brokenness and bitterness, because I chose to do things my own way. I carried a lot of unnecessary baggage into other relationships and for that reason, the relationship failed. All the while God knew what I needed; He was just waiting on me. I always longed to have a partner that would serve the Lord with me, but I never once asked God for it. You see, the thing about God is that He gives us what we need and not what we want. Fortunately for me, God sent me the most amazing man, but first I had to get to know God on a deeper, spiritual level. I needed to find out who I was first, I needed to forgive people who have hurt me so badly, and most important of all, I had to forgive myself. And in doing so, I was healed from my past and I discovered a love greater than anyone would ever know or understand, unless you have God in your life.

God took me through this process of healing and self-discovery, it happened in the strangest way, one I never saw coming. But that is just how God works, in ways we cannot see or will ever understand. All I had to do was to be willing and obedient. God sometimes sends people our way to help us, or even just to give us a message, and we as the humans we are, choose to ignore it, not knowing or realizing that it could have been our moment, but we chose to be ignorant and disobedient. We must have a willingness to act on the things God shows us.

We need to have a Father, Son and Holy Spirit relationship. We develop this by praying, (talking to God) asking Him to come into our lives, our hearts. Seeking His guidance, wisdom and knowledge.

What God desires to give us before a person:
·   Place

He desires to put in you a place where He knows purpose can happen in your life. (We all have a purpose in life- we are here for a reason).

· Purpose

Know what your purpose is, God speaks to us in many ways, through signs, dreams, visions, and people. When you have the Holy Spirit within you, you will know when it comes from God. We can commit to obeying the things God wants us to do in life, so that we can live a righteous life honors Him. We can make decisions with God as our source of wisdom and discernment. Romans 8:14 For as many as are led by the Spirit of God, there are sons of God.

· Provision

God only funds His plans, in other words, where God guides, He provides. He grants us provision for the things we need to pursue. He gives us what we need and not what we want. So wherever God is taking you, He will make sure you have everything you need.

· Identity

Know who you are in Christ. As explained in Chapter one, you can only know who you are, if you know God. Isaiah 43:1 Fear not for I have redeemed you, I have called you by name, you are mine. Psalm 139:14 You are fearfully and wonderfully made. Genesis 1:27 You were created in His image.

· Parameters

If you do not set standards, your relationship will not

work. 1 Corinthians 10:23 I have the right to do anything you say, but not everything is beneficial. I have the right to do anything, but not everything is constructive. 2 Peter 2-3 Grace and peace be yours in abundance through the knowledge of God and of Jesus our Lord. His divine power has given us everything we need for a godly life through our knowledge of Him who called us by His own glory and goodness. If God's not enough, no person will ever be.

Eye hath not seen, nor ear heard, neither have entered into the heart of man, the things which God hath prepared for them that love Him   1 Corinthians 2:9

Chapter Five

"C.C.C

."Make the Choice, take the Chance, be the Change.

Making the Choice:

We all desire the beautiful things in life but are we willing to wait for it? We all desire to be loved, to be adored, appreciated and accepted. But what if it is not meant to happen now? What if we need to go through a process, learn a few lessons, before we get what we want? Sometimes we pray for something, and we expect God to answer immediately, but God's plan is not ours. God sometimes makes us wait, because we might not be ready for what He wants to give us. The process might be long and painful at times, but it is God's way of preparing us for what lies ahead. There might be something in your future that might require you to be strong, so the process is there to help you grow and to make us stronger. Ephesians 3:20 God is able to do exceedingly abundantly above all that we ask or think. So, this is why waiting on the Lord is the only way to a fulfilled future.

So why not make that choice, choose God and whatever you ask in His name He will do for you. Choose to wait on the Lord.

Taking the Chance:

It is not always easy doing the right thing, but it is worth it in the end. There is so much peace in knowing that you have done everything that God has desired of you. We grew up in a world where sex before marriage is normal. Loving with a partner and not being married is normal. Having a child at the age of sixteen is normal and yet it is not what God wants for us. The Bible teaches us just the opposite. We choose this way because we see things being done this way and, in some cases, because others are doing it and it is so much easier than to wait.

Finding a partner and having to wait for them, seems frustrating and at times you get disheartened, tired even. But waiting on God makes it all worthwhile. It has a lot to do with who you are in Christ and setting boundaries for yourself. So why not take that chance and choose to be different, imagine the kind of children you will bring into this world. They become better adults, make better choices. Our kids learn from us. Take that chance and trust God with your future. Proverbs 3:5-6 Trust in the Lord will all your heart and lean not on your own understanding. In all your ways acknowledge Him and He will direct your paths.

Being the Change:

It is normal to always want to fit in with the crowd, but what if you decide to be different? To want to stand out. You will never whether the decisions you made changed someone else's life. Those are the things the things to pray for and to look for in a partner. Someone that shares in your interests, beliefs and passion. Someone that can help you grow, that supports our vision. Be someone that others can look up to and admire. God's love is constant, and it never runs out, once you experience it, you will have so much that it will overflow, and you can pour into others lives. People will look at you and not understand what it is about you, some will want of what you have. Make positive decisions and positivity will follow you. 1 John 4:16 God is love and all who live in love, live in God, and God lives in them. God is love and he who abides in love, abides in God, and God in him.

The Lord taketh pleasure in them that fear Him, in those that hope in His mercy Psalm 147:11

Chapter Six

"There will be storms"

What are storms? As defined by the dictionary – a violent disturbance of the atmosphere with strong winds and usually rain, thunder, lightning or snow. We can compare this to the many trials, uphill battles, frustration and anger we face from time to time. When we go through these storms, we often feel defeated, at a loss or hopeless. But what if the storms came to teach us something? (Important lessons) what if they came to clear the path for us?

When you live a life devoted to Christ you are often faced with these storms. Sometimes you will feel like this is it, it is the end. But you see the thing about storms is, they do not last. Storms are temporary, they are conversions of natural currents, in other words they are ever changing, they are natural. They will always be there, but with each storm we face, we learn how to overcome, and we become wiser, stronger.

God has a plan for your life, and He wants to make sure that you are well-equipped to fit in with the plan. The storms in our lives come to only make us stronger.

Our blessings come in seasons and like everything else, seasons come and go. Storms point us to God, when things are not going well in our lives, we tend to ask God why. We pray for it to pass. It is a time when we seem to seek God the most. That is why sometimes God sends storms to get our attention, to get us to draw closer to Him.

How to rise above the storm:
-        Believe you are built for storms- you can overcome them.

-        Know that storms are natural- they come and go

-        Understand the nature of storms- why they occur

-        Do not curse the storm – learn to understand it and use it

-        Use the storm to test your true self – what you believe in, your strengths and your weaknesses

-        Let the storms expand the limits of your potential – Ephesians 4:13 I can do all things through Christ who strengthens me.

-        Use the storm to test your faith in God

-        Let the storms clean out your relationships and your habits – develop a habit of prayer.

-        Build your house on the right foundation – The Word of God.

-        See the storm as a message from God.

The Name of the Lord is a strong tower; the righteous run into it and is safe.Proverbs 18:10

Chapter Seven

"God's timing"

Just because something doesn't make sense now, does not mean it does not make sense. It only means that you are not in the season or space where God makes sense of it.

We all go through struggles sometimes and at times we do not understand it. We question God on many occasions and at times it seems as if God is not listening, or He is not coming through for us. But in that time when God is silent, He is busy working in our lives. Our blessings will never arrive too early or too late. God is always on time. Isaiah 60:22 When the time is right, I, the Lord, will make it happen.

God's perfect timing does two things, it grows our faith as we are forced to wait and trust in God, and it also makes certain that He and He alone gets the glory and the praise for getting us through.

Sometimes delays from God can also be that He is protecting you. It's not always easy to wait but there is always a reason. Isaiah 40:13 They that wait on the Lord shall renew their strength. God sometimes makes us wait to grow us and to strengthen us, because there is something in our future that requires us to be strong, we should only trust the process.

In scripture the word wait, means to hope, to anticipate

and to trust. Our hope is in the Name of the Lord. To hope and to trust in the Lord requires faith, patience, humility and keeping the commandments. Exodus 20:2-17 and enduring to the end.

To wait on the Lord is to plant the seed of faith and nourish it.

To wait upon the Lord means taking your focus away from everything else and consider only the One true, living God. Fix your eyes upon Jesus, He is the Way, Truth and the Life. No one comes to the Father except through Him. John 14:6.

Being confident of this very thing, that He which hath begun a good work in you will perform it until the day of Jesus Christ Philippians 1:16

Chapter Eight

"Season of loneliness"

Nobody wants to be alone. We all desire to have someone with whom we can share everything. We long to be loved, comforted, reassured and understood.

But it is in our season of loneliness that God wants to use us, where we discover who and what we are in Christ, it is not so much being lonely but having to be alone. When you are in Christ you never feel lonely, for when you bear the fruits of the Spirit, it fills a void no one else can fill.

1. Love

The Hebrew word for love is pronounced (kheh-sed), which means undeserved kindness and generosity. The love that is willing to serve others. The type of love that makes it possible for believers to be at peace with one another. 1 Corinthians 13:4-13.

2. Joy

Joy is happiness produced by the Divine, unchanging nature of the promises of God and by Spiritual realities. We know that walking with God, the journey is not always pleasant and yet we find joy in them supernaturally by means of the Holy Spirit. Joy is a gift from God, and as believers we should delight in the blessing we already possess. Romans 15:13

3. Peace

Peace is that calm feeling we experience when God, by His

grace, calls us into His family and the Bible makes that possible for us. Religion can never give this to you, only Christ can give you deep-down peace. Philippians 4:6-7

4.   Longsuffering/ Patience

This is defined as the ability and willingness to endure painful, "irritating" circumstances, as well as injuries caused by others. Ephesians 5:2, Colossians 3:10. 1 Timothy 1:15-16.

5.   Kindness

This refers to the tenderness manifested in someone when he or she treats others with respect and consideration. Matthew 11:28-29. Matthew 19:13-14

6.   Goodness

It is the excellence in character shown through means of works of kindness.

Mark 10:18

7.   Faithfulness

Refers to being loyal and trustworthy. Our Lord shows us how to be faithful in His word. 1John 1:19

8.   Gentleness

This means we show tenderness and consideration for others. Also being submissive to God, seeking no revenge.

9.   Self-control

This means we must not follow after impulses or unholy desires. We must always stay of sober mind.

 God wants us to be solely focused on Him and in doing so we find that we often get tested by God. God wants to see if we can make it on our own, sometimes our purpose requires us to go through a period of being alone. Being alone teaches you to be strong, because there's no one else around at the time that you can rely on, but yourself and your own strength. It is very important to seek God first in this time, to call on Him for strength and wisdom.

God never intended for us to be alone. Genesis 2:18 The Lord God said, "It is not good for man to be alone. I will make a helper suitable for him". It is also a process of self-discovery (finding our true selves).

According to the dictionary, the word loneliness means sadness because one has no friends or company. Loneliness can be experienced whether alone or even in a room full of people. It is what we feel inside. But are we ever truly alone? No, God is always with us. When we seek His presence, when we call upon His Name. He is there with us; He surrounds us with His everlasting love and fills our hearts with His peace. The peace that surpasses all understanding. Philippians 4:7.

A life lived without Christ is an empty life. We all in our lives have experienced some kind of loneliness and it makes us stronger people, but having Christ through all of it, makes us even stronger. Deuteronomy 31:8 The Lord Himself goes before you, He will never leave you, nor forsake you. Do not be afraid: do not be discouraged.

So, if you find yourself in a season of loneliness, know that God has a reason for it. God takes us through a season of loneliness, so we can learn to love ourselves.

When we are alone, God has an opportunity to speak to us, to get our undivided attention. Being by yourself means more time for yourself, focusing on your inner self, your abilities, your dreams, your visions and also most importantly, focusing on your relationship with God.

Loneliness can be used to develop our character. Paul said: "when I am weak, I am strong. When we are alone our commitment is tested and our true character shines through. Being faithful alone gives us confidence, we can be faithful to others.

Why does God allow us to be lonely?

·	He uses it to turn our attention to Him.
Seek Him first in all things. Let your intimate relationship with God be your most precious treasure.

·	He uses it to develop your skills in reaching out to others first. If you desire to have friends, you need to be a friend too. (self-love)

·	He uses it to help other lonely people. You develop a sensitivity and understanding for other lonely people. These kinds of people become attracted to you.

·	He uses it to teach you how to think. We become so busy with our lives that we hardly have a moment to think. Teach yourself to have a positive mindset, ask God's guidance and to remove all doubt, fear and anxiety from your heart and mind. Fill your mind with God's word and everything positive. Find quiet time with God and reflect over your past failures and learn to correct certain habits.

·	He uses it to prepare you for your calling/vision/purpose.
God's ideas and methods do not always blend well with the world's way of doing things, which is why it's important to spend time alone with God, to learn His ways and His thoughts.

Now the God of hope fill you with all joy and peace in believing that ye may abound in hope, through the power of the Holy spirit
Romans 15:13